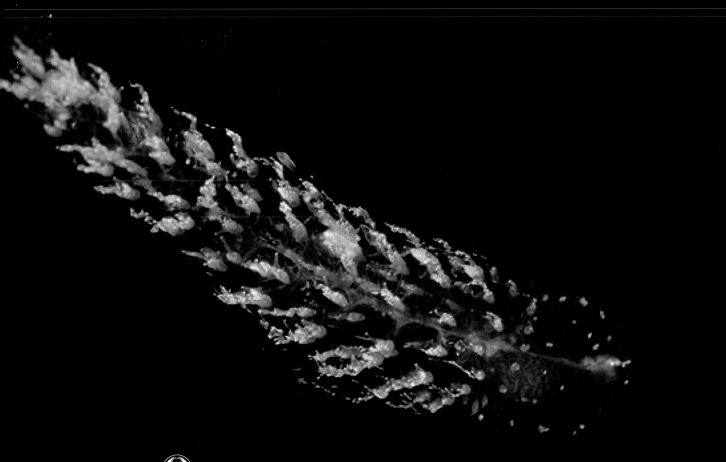

A FIREFLY BOOK

Published by Firefly Books Ltd. 2020
First published by Red Bird Publishing Ltd., U.K.
Copyright © 2020 Red Bird Publishing Ltd., U.K.
Text © Lisa Regan
All images used under license from Shutterstock.com

First printing

Library of Congress Control Number: 2020934085

Library and Archives Canada Cataloguing in Publication
Title: Glow down deep : amazing creatures that light up / Lisa Regan.
Names: Regan, Lisa, 1971- author.
Identifiers: Canadiana 20200199501 | ISBN 9780228102533 (hardcover) | ISBN 9780228102526 (softcover)
Subjects: LCSH: Bioluminescence—Juvenile literature. | LCSH: Biofluorescence—Juvenile literature. |
   LCSH: Marine animals—Behavior—Juvenile literature. | LCSH: Marine organisms—Juvenile literature.
Classification: LCC QH641 .R43 2020 | DDC j572/.4358—dc23

Published in Canada by
Firefly Books Ltd.
50 Staples Avenue, Unit 1
Richmond Hill, Ontario
L4B 0A7

Published in the United States by
Firefly Books (U.S.) Inc.
P.O. Box 1338, Ellicott Station
Buffalo, New York
14205

Printed in China

Glow
Down Deep

Amazing Creatures That Light Up

Written by Lisa Regan

FIREFLY BOOKS

Contents

Biofluorescence
Creatures that biofluoresce (say it: by-oh-fluh-ress) absorb light and then give it out again when they need to. They take in natural blue light and emit it in different ways, usually as a green, red or orange glow.

Bioluminescence

Bioluminescence (say it: by-oh-loo-min-ess-uns) is sometimes called living light, as the creatures and other organisms make it within their own bodies. It is caused by a **chemical reaction** that is much like cracking a glow stick to make it light up.

Lights Out!

The marine world is full of living things that glow in the dark. Coral reefs, fish, jelly creatures of all shapes and sizes…if you shine a violet light on them, you will see them light up with vivid neon shades. Some creatures can even flash their own homemade lights to attract a **mate** or hide from an enemy. Scientists now know of more and more organisms that light up in the darkness; some think around ninety percent of sea creatures do it. Explore these fascinating light shows for yourself with pages full of glowing wonders of the world!

*Look for the **highlighted** words in the glossary at the back of the book.*

When you see a ☆, hold the book under a light source for thirty seconds. Then turn off the lights to see the pages glow!

Glowing Ocean

The beautiful blue glow of this water is sometimes known as sea sparkle. It is caused by millions of microscopic creatures known as Noctiluca scintillans (say it: nok-tee-loo-kah sin-til-ans). They are common in many coastal areas and can gather in thick, scummy masses that look pink or red in the daytime. They float near the surface and flash brightly if they are disturbed, by the waves, boats, or even by people walking along the shore.

DID YOU KNOW?

Some creatures swallow so much of this bioluminescent plankton that they themselves begin to glow.

Comb Jelly

These soft-bodied sea creatures look like jellyfish but are in a scientific group of their own. They get their name from the comb-like lines of cilia (say it: silly-uh) that move in waves to help push the comb jelly through the water. The main body of the jelly is see-through but they have **bioluminescent** parts that can produce their own light if they are touched.

Comb jellies are ancient creatures that have lived in the oceans for at least 500 million years. They can be different shapes and sizes. Some have long **tentacles** while others are sack-shaped with a very large mouth that they can fasten shut really tightly.

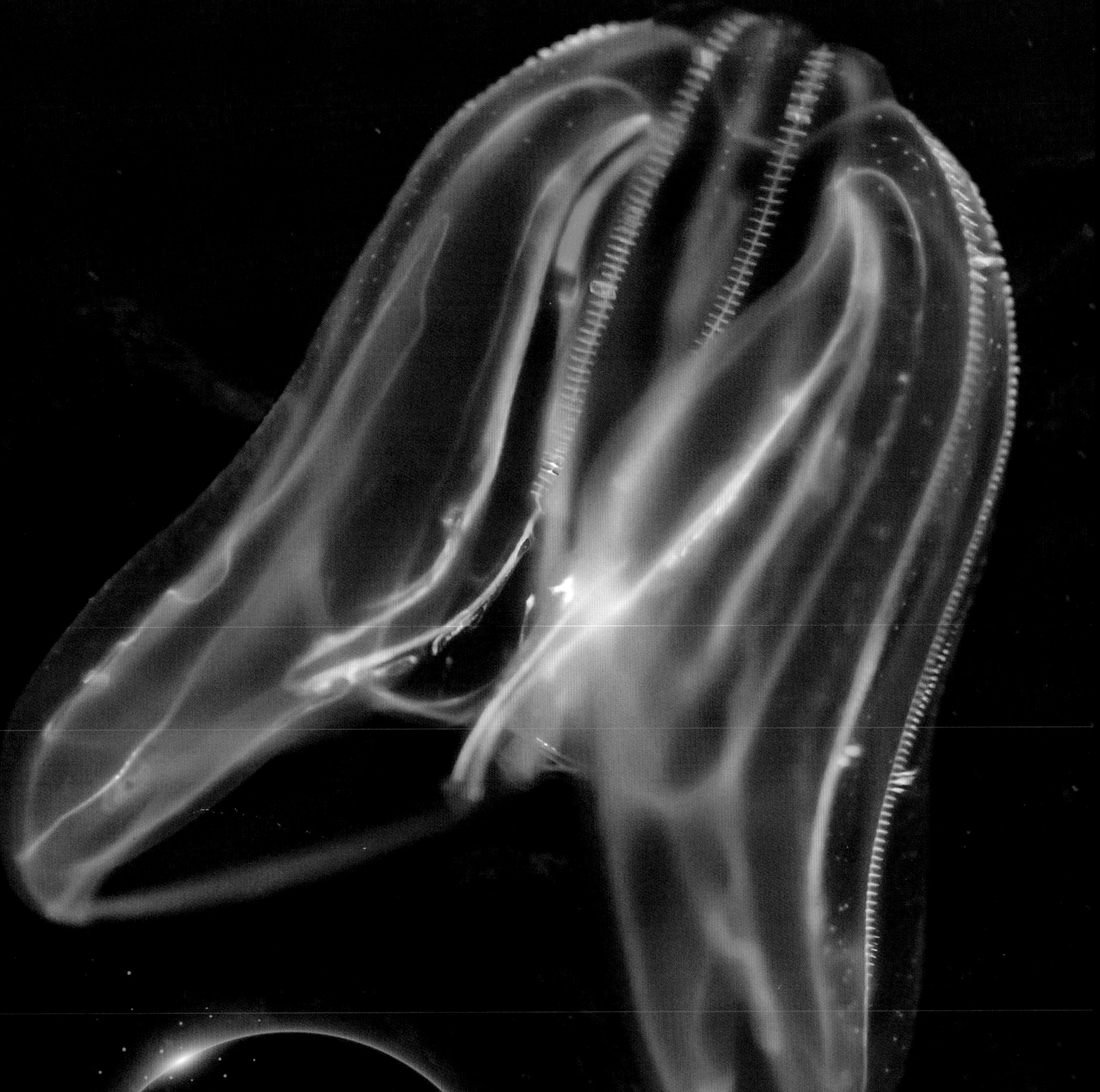

DID YOU KNOW?

Comb jellies belong to a group called ctenophores (say it: ten-uh-forz). There are about 100–150 known species.

Dragonfish

Look at this beast! It is a dragonfish, and it lives deep in the sea where very little light reaches. They can easily live 1.6 km (1 mile) below the surface and have been found in all the world's oceans. They feed on jellyfish and have extremely large teeth compared to their body size. These teeth are sharp, backward-facing **fangs** that trap food inside the fish's mouth.

Dragonfish have sensitive **barbels** that can sense movement around them. One even longer barbel on its chin has a bioluminescent light on the end that attracts **prey** and possibly other dragonfish for mating.

Siphonophore

These long, trailing sea constructions create their own light whenever they bump into something. Giant siphonophores (say it: sy-fon-uh-forz) are only skinny—around the same width as a baseball bat handle—but reach lengths of 40 m (130 feet), which is even longer than a blue whale. Their body is jelly-like and often see-through for most of its length.

DID
YOU KNOW?

A siphonophore is actually
a collection of lots of
individual creatures
clinging together
in a colony.

Siphonophores have a varied diet of baby fish, tiny
crustaceans (say it: krus-tay-shunz) and other jelly
animals which they grab with their **tentacles**

Glowing Coral

Corals might look like plants but they actually contain lots of tiny animals known as **polyps** (say it: paw-lips). These creatures build a hard outer shell from limestone to protect their soft body. They are related to anemones and jellyfish and are mostly nocturnal, feeding during the night time. They have **algae** living inside that supply the corals with nutrients. Shallow water corals use fluorescence to protect them from the sun, like sunscreen. Deeper water corals most likely fluoresce to help the algae make food from sunlight.

DID YOU KNOW?

A polyp's mouth is surrounded by stingers called nematocysts (say it: ni-mat-uh-sists) which it uses to grab food as it floats or swims past.

Cock-Eyed Squid

One of this creature's eyes is unexceptional, but the other one is almost twice the size and looks too big for the creature's body. It is also yellow and bulges out of the squid's head. Scientists think it uses this large eye to spot creatures that are hiding with their own bioluminescence. The yellow acts as a filter to see past the blue light.

The squid's red body is covered with darker dots and speckles which give off their own light. They are known as **photophores** (say it: foh-tuh-forz) and earn the squid its nickname of jewel squid as they glow with brilliant, shimmering shades of blue and green.

DID YOU KNOW?

Squid are in a group of mollusks known as cephalopods (say it: sef-uh -luh-podz) that also includes octopuses.

Sea Pen

Named after the old-fashioned quill pens made of feathers, the sea pen is a type of sea creature known as a cnidarian (say it: ny-dair-ee-un). They lodge themselves on the sea floor with a bulb-like anchor called a peduncle. Their frills, almost like branches, are **polyps** consisting of a hollow stalk with a mouth and **tentacles** at the end.

DID YOU KNOW?

Sea pens can make themselves bigger by taking in water and then smaller again by pushing it out.

The sea pen's tentacles make waves of green bioluminescent light that flash from the base to the end of the creature. They are mostly static creatures but they can uproot and move to a new position if necessary to find the right currents to push food past their tentacles.

Bigfin Reef Squid

Named for the fin that runs around the outside edge of its whole body, this squid often gathers in groups called shoals. They are eaten by large **predators** such as dolphin and tuna. Their basic body coloring is white but they have a variety of **cells** that allow them to change pattern and color, often really quickly. They can produce their own shiny red and green shades, and can also reflect back light from around them. Like all squid, bigfin reef squid have eight arms and two long **tentacles.**

DID YOU KNOW?

These squid grow faster than most other types of squid and are of great interest to marine biologists.

Krill

These tiny shrimp-like creatures are sometimes nicknamed light shrimp because they are bioluminescent. They have lights on sections of their body, and also on the end of their long eyestalks! Krill are one of the animals that use **counter-illumination** to hide from their **predators**. They light up on their underside to break up their outline, hiding against the pale surface of the water so they can't be seen from below.

DID YOU KNOW?

Scientists have named over 100 types of krill and they are found in all of the world's oceans, even the Antarctic.

Krill are not much bigger than a paper clip, but there are billions of them in the ocean. They feed near the surface on microscopic plants known as phytoplankton (say it: fy-toh-plank-tun) and are themselves a really important food source for fish, penguins, seals, and whales.

Crystal Jellyfish

Hat-shaped and beautiful, crystal jellyfish have around 150 **tentacles** that form a frill around their edge. Each tentacle has venomous threads known as nematocysts (say it: ni-mat-uh-sists) that are used for capturing **prey**. A crystal jellyfish is harmless to humans and is only around the size of your open hand. Its body is almost see-through but has a blue glowing ring around its outer edge.

DID YOU KNOW?

Crystal jellyfish catch and eat small floating creatures including other crystal jellyfish! It has an expanding mouth so it can eat animals half its own size.

These blue **cells** are coated with a green fluorescent substance that immediately absorbs blue light and turns it green. It transforms the crystal jelly into a green blinking UFO when prodded.

Sea Cucumber

This creature is a good example of what scientists call the "burglar alarm" effect. The sea cucumber produces lots of bioluminescent light to draw attention to the fact it is being attacked. The bright light attracts other creatures which act almost like the police, frightening off the **predators** and allowing the sea cucumber to get away. Sea cucumbers are echinoderms (say it: eck-in-oh-durmz) which means they are related to sea urchins, sand dollars, and sea stars (starfish).

DID YOU KNOW?

Some sea cucumbers can detach their bioluminescent body parts to act as a distraction and allow them to escape from prey.

Helmet Jellyfish

26

Bell-shaped jellyfish like this one are known as Medusae (say it: meh-doo-sy), after the mythological character that has dangling snakes instead of hair.

The helmet jellyfish has a red body and twelve **tentacles**. It swims by contracting and expanding its body to push water behind it and propel itself forward. Its body can grow to 30 cm (1 ft) long.

These creatures use their red bioluminescent flashes to communicate with each other. They may also be used to confuse their **predators**.

They also light up if they are touched, and will produce rippling waves of light along their body.

False Stonefish

This fish is so well camouflaged that it looks exactly like the stony seabed it lurks on. Its bumpy skin can take on the patterns and blotches of the sand, and it lies so still that **algae** grows on it. It has side fins that can be fanned out to warn off its enemies.

A false stonefish biofluorescent, but th biofluorescence is only visibl in blue or ultraviolet light. Th stonefish's whole body reflect the light back as a re shimmer. The fluorescer patterns are probabl used by the fish t communicate wit each other, and mak them difficult fc other fish to see

Anglerfish

Don't be fooled by this picture: these fish are tiny. Even the largest females would fit on the palm of your hand.

The strange light on top of this fish's head is an adapted dorsal fin spine. It glows white because of bioluminescence, but not from the fish itself. Instead, **bacteria** on the end of the spine give off light, which the fish uses to attract **prey** toward its mouth. It lives in the very deepest parts of the ocean (as much as 3,000 m/9,800 feet) where there is no other light. They are sometimes nicknamed sea devils because of their frightening appearance.

Pipefish

This long, skinny fish is a relative of seahorses and seadragons. It has the same tiny mouth and long snout with no teeth. Like seahorses, it isn't a very good swimmer, and floats with the current. Many of them use their tail to hold on tightly to seaweed when they want to stay in one place.

Pipefish don't grow very big. The small ones are around 7 cm (3 in) and the longest are only up to 20 cm (8 in).

One type, the dragonface pipefish, has orange glowing lines down its head and body. The biofluorescent messmate pipefish re-emits blue light as yellow. Many of them have rings and ridges down their body, formed from their skeleton.

Plankton

Some plankton are tiny plants and are called phytoplankton (say it: fy-toh-plank-tun). However, others are small creatures, such as fish eggs and **larvae**, tiny shellfish known as copepods (say it: koh-pee-podz) and single-celled animals called dinoflagellates (say it: dy-noh-fla-juh-lutz). These are known together as zooplankton.

Plankton make bioluminescent light when they are agitated (moved more quickly than normal). Like other bioluminescent creatures, they do it by mixing two chemicals together to produce a glow. The chemical that makes the light is called a luciferin (say it: loo-sif-er-in) and the one that causes the **chemical reaction** is the luciferase (say it: loo-sif-er-ayz).

DID YOU KNOW?

Strictly speaking, plankton are not strong enough to swim against a current, although some of them are able to swim by themselves, weakly.

35

White-Spotted Jellyfish

Often found in large swarms, these jellyfish can gobble up so much **plankton** that other creatures are left without food. Their white spots and eight thick arms shine in the dark. They live for around a year and are strong swimmers compared to some other jellyfish.

White-spotted jellyfish prefer warm water and can be seen in coastal shallows. They grow to around 50 cm (20 in) across, although some get much bigger. They are venomous but their sting is so mild you may not notice you have been stung.

Hatchetfish

DID YOU KNOW?

Many hatchetfish have tube-shaped eyes that permanently point upward to look for the silhouette of their prey overhead.

Lots of deep-sea creatures hunt by looking above them to catch sight of creatures outlined in the faintly-lit waters. To avoid becoming **prey** themselves, hatchetfish use **counter-illumination**. They make bioluminescent light on their underside so that **predators** looking up will see a glow rather than a dark outline.

Hatchetfish don't grow particularly big. Many are only 3 cm (1.2 in) long, and even the giant hatchetfish only reaches 12 cm (4.7 in), and would fit on your outstretched hand.

Chain Catshark

This small shark has been caught on camera in the water near Mexico. It is biofluorescent, so absorbs light and re-emits it as a green glow. It even has biofluorescent molecules in its eyes! It hides in rock crevices at the bottom of the ocean where only blue light can reach.

The chain catshark has beautiful reddish-brown skin and darker, chain-like markings that are visible in ordinary white light. Their fluorescence is only visible to humans in a special light, but it helps the sharks see each other easily in the murky depths of the ocean.

DID YOU KNOW?

Scientists have found over 200 species of fish that use biofluorescence, but only four of them so far are sharks.

Bobtail Squid

The bobtail squid has a light **organ** on its body that is home to bioluminescent **bacteria**. These bacteria feed on sugars produced by the squid, and in return they help the squid to hide while it hunts at night. The glow given off by the bacteria matches the moonlight above the water, and its brightness can be controlled by the squid.

DID YOU KNOW?

One species of bobtail squid is nicknamed the fire shooter, as it squirts a glowing cloud to confuse its predators.

42

This tiny, thumb-sized squid has been sent into space! Scientists wanted to study the effects on the bacteria of being in a reduced gravity environment. In the wild, the squid swap their bacteria every day, taking on a new batch to light their way the following night.

Tube Anemone

Tube anemones look similar to sea anemones, and are related to them, but they are a different type of creature. They are one of the oldest animals on the planet, going back to around 600 million years ago. Only sponges and comb jellies are older.

DID YOU KNOW?

A tube anemone's feeding tentacles grow longer in the darkness! They grab small food particles that float past.

A tube anemone has two rings of fluorescent tentacles, up to 200 altogether. The outer ones have stinging **cells** for catching food. The inner ring is often a different shade, and its tentacles pull food into its central mouth. They bury themselves in soft sand or mud but can move from place to place if they need to. They can also withdraw into a tube for protection.

Viperfish

DID YOU KNOW?

A viperfish hunts by charging into other fish, and it has a special bone behind its head that acts like an airbag.

A fierce **predator** with a large mouth, this deep-sea fish doesn't grow particularly big. Even the largest are only around 30 cm (1 foot) long. Its curved, backward-pointing **fangs**, however, are huge for its body size and don't fully fit inside its mouth. It has a long spine on its back with a bioluminescent **organ** on the end, which it flashes on and off to attract smaller fish. It also has rows of **photophores** along its sides which may help it to hide or to communicate with other viperfish.

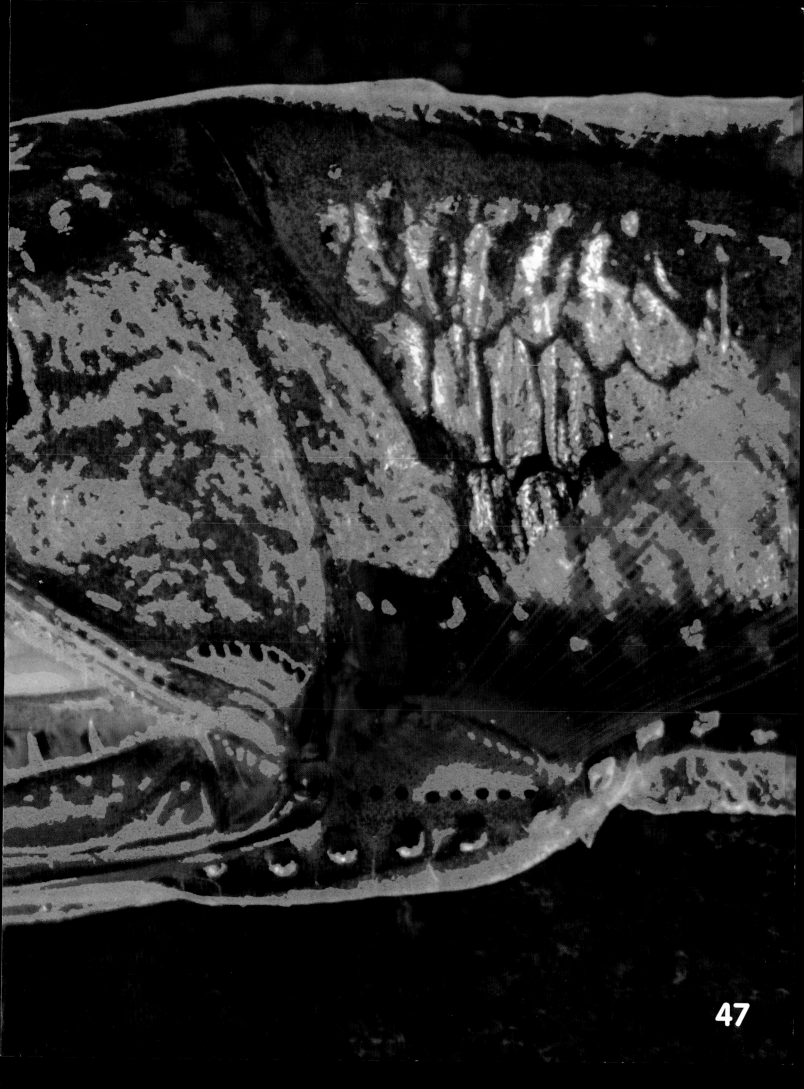